Books by Paul Zindel

The Pigman
Outstanding Children's Books of 1968, *The New York Times*
Notable Children's Books, 1940–1970 (ALA)
Best of the Best for Young Adults, 1966–1988 (ALA)

My Darling, My Hamburger
Outstanding Children's Books of 1969, *The New York Times*

I Never Loved Your Mind
Outstanding Children's Books of 1970, *The New York Times*

The Effect of Gamma Rays on Man-in-the-Moon Marigolds
1971 Pulitzer Prize for Drama
Best American Play of 1970 (New York Drama Desk
Critics Circle Award)
Notable Books of 1971 (ALA)
Best of the Best for Young Adults 1966–1988 (ALA)

I Love My Mother
(a picture book, illustrated by John Melo)

Pardon Me, You're Stepping On My Eyeball!
Outstanding Children's Books of 1976, *The New York Times*
Best Books for Young Adults, 1976 (ALA)

Confessions of a Teenage Baboon
Best Books for Young Adults, 1977 (ALA)

The Undertaker's Gone Bananas

The Pigman's Legacy
Outstanding Children's Books of 1980, *The New York Times*
Best Books for Young Adults, 1980 (ALA)

A Star for the Latecomer
(with Bonnie Zindel)

The Girl Who Wanted a Boy

Harry and Hortense at Hormone High

To Take a Dare
(with Crescent Dragonwagon)
Best Books for Young Adults, 1982 (ALA)

The Amazing and Death-Defying Diary of Eugene Dingman
(A Charlotte Zolotow Book)
1988 Book for the Teen Age (New York Public Library)

A Begonia for Miss Applebaum
(A Charlotte Zolotow Book)
Best Books for Young Adults, 1989 (ALA)
1990 Book for the Teen Age (New York Public Library)

The Pigman & Me
(A Charlotte Zolotow Book)

THE EFFECT
OF GAMMA RAYS
ON
MAN-IN-THE-MOON MARIGOLDS

THE EFFECT OF GAMMA RAYS

A Drama in Two Acts

drawings

ON MAN-IN-THE-MOON MARIGOLDS

by Paul Zindel

by Dong Kingman

HarperCollins*Publishers*

LIBRARY OF CONGRESS CATALOG CARD NUMBER: 79-135772
ISBN 0-06-026829-8

To Betty Frank

Marigolds was written when I was twenty-five years old. One morning I awoke and discovered the manuscript next to my typewriter. I suspect it is autobiographical, because whenever I see a production of it I laugh and cry harder than anyone else in the audience. I laugh because the play always reminds me of still another charmingly frantic scheme of my mother's to get rich quick—a profusion of schemes all of which couldn't possibly appear in the play: It might be the time my mother decided to make a fortune as a dog breeder but ended up with twenty-six collies when no buyers appeared; or perhaps I'll recall her hot dog emporium at a small airport; or her Phone-A-Gift Service. I remember an endless series of preposterous undertakings—hatcheck girl, PT boat riveter, unlicensed real estate broker.

But my tears come from a time several years after the play was written, when I returned to my mother's house knowing she had only a few months to live; she was unaware of the fact that she was dying. We had long before made that peace between parent and son which Nature insists not happen until the teen years have passed. During that privileged time just before she died, we enjoyed each other as friends. If she felt strong on a particular day she'd ask to go for a car ride. She loved burnt-almond ice cream, shrimp in lobster sauce, and flowers in bloom. On one of our trips we discovered a grove with a family of pheasants, a floor of lilies of the valley, and a ceiling of wisteria. Always we talked of the past—of her father, of his vegetable wagon in old Stapleton, of a man who rented a room in her father's house in which to store thousands of Christmas toys. There was always the unusual, the hilarity, the sadness. In her own way she told me of her secret dreams and fears—so many of which somehow I had sensed, and discovered written into that manuscript next to my typewriter, many years before.

Paul Zindel

THE EFFECT

OF GAMMA RAYS

ON

MAN-IN-THE-MOON MARIGOLDS

CHARACTERS

TILLIE:
The Girl

"In front of my eyes, one part of the world was becoming another. Atoms exploding . . . atom after atom breaking down into something new . . . It would go on for millions of years . . ."

BEATRICE:
The Mother

"This long street, with all the doors of the houses shut and everything crowded next to each other . . . And then I start getting afraid that the vegetables are going to spoil . . . and that nobody's going to buy anything . . ."

RUTH:
The Other
Daughter

"Well, they say I came out of my room . . . and I started down the stairs, step by step . . . and I heard the choking and banging on the bed . . ."

NANNY   . . .

JANICE
VICKERY   . . .

THE SETTING

A room of wood which was once a vegetable store—
and a point of debarkation for a horse-drawn wagon
to bring its wares to a small town.

But the store is gone, and a widow of confusion has
placed her touch on everything. A door to NANNY's
room leads off from this main room, and in front of

the door hang faded curtains which allow ventilation in the summer. There is a hallway and a telephone.

A heavy wood staircase leads to a landing with a balustrade, two doors, and a short hall. BEATRICE sleeps in one room; TILLIE and RUTH share the other.

Objects which respectable people usually hide in closets are scattered about the main room: newspapers, magazines, dishes; empty bottles; clothes; suitcases; last week's sheets. Such carelessness is the type which is so perfected it must have evolved from hereditary processes; but in all fairness to the occupants, it can be pointed out that after twilight, when shadows and weak bulbs work their magic, the room becomes interesting.

On a table near the front left of the room is a small wire cage designed to hold a rabbit. Near this are several school books, notebook papers, and other weapons of high school children. A kitchen area, boasting a hot plate, has been carved near the bottom of the staircase, and the window, which was formerly the front of the vegetable store, is now mostly covered with old newspapers so that passers-by cannot see in. A bit of the clear glass remains at the top—but drab, lifeless drapes line the sides of the window.

DONG KINGMAN

ACT I

The lights go down slowly as music creeps in—a theme for lost children, the near misbegotten.
From the blackness TILLIE'S VOICE *speaks against the music.*

TILLIE'S VOICE: He told me to look at my hand, for a part of it came from a star that exploded too long ago to imagine. This part of me was formed from a tongue of fire that screamed through the heavens until there was our sun. And this part of me—this tiny part of me —was on the sun when it itself exploded and whirled in a great storm until the planets came to be.

Lights start in.

And this small part of me was then a whisper of the earth. When there was life, perhaps this part of me got lost in a fern that was crushed and covered until it was coal. And then it was a diamond millions of years later—it must have been a diamond

1

as beautiful as the star from which it had first come.

TILLIE: *Taking over from recorded voice.*
Or perhaps this part of me became lost in a terrible beast, or became part of a huge bird that flew above the primeval swamps.

And he said this thing was so small —this part of me was so small it couldn't be seen—but it was there from the beginning of the world.

And he called this bit of me an atom. And when he wrote the word, I fell in love with it.
Atom.
Atom.
What a beautiful word.

The phone rings.

BEATRICE: *Off stage.*
Will you get that please?

The phone rings again before BEA-
TRICE *appears in her bathrobe from
the kitchen.*

No help! Never any help!

She answers the phone.

Hello? Yes it is. Who is this? . . . I
hope there hasn't been any trouble
at school . . . Oh, she's always been
like that. She hardly says a word
around here, either. I always say
some people were born to speak and
others born to listen . . .

You know I've been meaning to call
you to thank you for that lovely rabbit you gave Matilda. She and I just
adore it and it's gotten so big . . .

Well, it certainly was thoughtful.
Mr. Goodman, I don't mean to
change the subject but aren't you
that delightful young man Tillie
said hello to a couple of months back

at the A & P? You were by the lobster tank and I was near the frozen foods? That delightful and handsome young man? . . . Why, I would very much indeed use the expression *handsome*. Yes, and . . .

Well, I encourage her at every opportunity at home. Did she say I didn't? Both my daughters have their own desks and I put 75-watt bulbs right near them . . . Yes . . . Yes . . . I think those tests are very much overrated, anyway, Mr. Goodman . . . Well, believe me she's nothing like that around this house . . .

Now I don't want you to think I don't appreciate what you're trying to do, Mr. Goodman, but I'm afraid it's simply useless. I've tried just everything, but she isn't a pretty girl —I mean, let's be frank about it— she's going to have her problems. Are you married, Mr. Goodman? Oh,

that's too bad. I don't know what's the matter with women today letting a handsome young man like you get away . . .

Well, some days she just doesn't feel like going to school. You just said how bright she is, and I'm really afraid to put too much of a strain on her after what happened to her sister. You know, too much strain is the worst thing in this modern world, Mr. Goodman, and I can't afford to have another convulsive on my hands, now can I? But don't you worry about Matilda. There will be some place for her in this world. And, like I said, some were born to speak and others just to listen . . . and do call again, Mr. Goodman. It's been a true pleasure speaking with you. Goodbye.

BEATRICE *hangs up the phone and advances into the main room. The lights come up.*

Matilda, that wasn't very nice of you to tell them I was forcibly detaining you from school. Why, the way that Mr. Goodman spoke, he must think I'm running a concentration camp. Do you have any idea how embarrassing it is to be accused of running a concentration camp for your own children?

Well, it isn't embarrassing at all.

That school of yours is forty years behind the times anyway, and believe me you learn more around here than that ugly Mr. Goodman can teach you!

You know, I really feel sorry for him. I never saw a man with a more effeminate face in my life. When I saw you talking to him by the lobster tank I said to myself, "Good Lord, for a science teacher my poor girl has got herself a Hebrew hermaphrodite." Of course, he's not as bad as

Miss Hanley. The idea of letting her teach girl's gym is staggering.

And you have to place me in the embarrassing position of giving them a reason to call me at eight-thirty in the morning, no less.

TILLIE: I didn't say anything.

BEATRICE: What do you tell them when they want to know why you stay home once in a while?

TILLIE: I tell them I'm sick.

BEATRICE: Oh, you're sick all right, the exact nature of the illness not fully realized, but you're sick all right. Any daughter that would turn her mother in as the administrator of a concentration camp has got to be suffering from something very peculiar.

TILLIE: Can I go in today, Mother?

BEATRICE: You'll go in, all right.

TILLIE: Mr. Goodman said he was going to do an experiment—

BEATRICE: Why, he looks like the kind that would do his experimenting after sundown.

TILLIE: On radioactivity—

BEATRICE: On radioactivity? That's all that high school needs!

TILLIE: He's going to bring in the cloud chamber—

BEATRICE: Why, what an outstanding event. If you had warned me yesterday I would've gotten all dressed to kill and gone with you today. I love seeing cloud chambers being brought in.

TILLIE: You can actually see—

BEATRICE: You're giving me a headache.

TILLIE: Please?

BEATRICE: No, my dear, the fortress of knowl-
            edge is not going to be blessed with
            your presence today. I have a good
            number of exciting duties for you
            to take care of, not the least of which
            is rabbit droppings.

TILLIE: Oh, Mother, please . . . I'll do it
            after school.

BEATRICE: If we wait a minute longer this house
            is going to ferment. I found rabbit
            droppings in my bedroom even.

TILLIE: I could do it after Mr. Goodman's
            class. I'll say I'm ill and ask for a
            sick pass.

BEATRICE: Do you want me to chloroform that
            thing right this minute?

TILLIE: No!

BEATRICE: Then shut up.

RUTH *comes to the top of the stairs. She is dressed for school, and though her clothes are simple she gives the impression of being slightly strange. Her hair isn't quite combed, her sweater doesn't quite fit, etc.*

RUTH: Do you have Devil's Kiss down there?

BEATRICE: It's in the bathroom cabinet.

RUTH *comes downstairs and goes to the bathroom door, located under the stairs. She flings it open and rummages in the cabinet.*

RUTH: There's so much junk in here it's driving me crazy.

BEATRICE: Maybe it's in my purse . . . If you don't hurry up you'll be late for school.

RUTH: Well, I couldn't very well go in without Devil's Kiss, now could I?

BEATRICE: Doesn't anyone go to school these days without that all over their lips?

RUTH: *Finding the lipstick.*
Nobody I know, except Tillie, that is. And if she had a little lipstick on I'll bet they wouldn't have laughed at her so much yesterday.

BEATRICE: Why were they laughing?

RUTH: The assembly. Didn't she tell you about the assembly?

BEATRICE: Ruth, you didn't tell me she was in an assembly.

RUTH: Well, I just thought of it right now. How could I tell you anything until I think of it—did you ever stop to consider that? Some crummy science assembly.

BEATRICE: *To* TILLIE.
What is she talking about?

RUTH: I thought she'd tell the whole world. Imagine, right in front of the assembly, with everybody laughing at her.

BEATRICE: Will you be quiet, Ruth? *Why were they laughing at you?*

TILLIE: I don't know.

RUTH: You don't know? My heavens, she was a sight. She had that old jumper on—the faded one with that low collar—and a raggy slip that showed all over and her hair looked like she was struck by lightning.

BEATRICE: You're exaggerating . . .

RUTH: She was cranking this model of something—

TILLIE: The atom.

RUTH: This model of the atom . . . you know, it had this crank and a long tower so that when you turned it these little colored balls went spinning around like crazy. And there was Tillie, cranking away, looking weird as a coot . . . that old jumper with the raggy slip and the lightning hair . . . cranking away while some boy with glasses was reading this stupid speech . . . and everybody burst into laughter until the teachers yelled at them. And all day long, the kids kept coming up to me saying, "Is that really your sister? How can you bear it?" And you know, Chris Burns says to me— "*She* looks like the one that went to the looney doctors." I could have kissed him there and then.

BEATRICE: *Taking a backscratcher.*
Matilda, if you can't get yourself dressed properly before going to school you're never going to go again. I don't like the idea of everybody laughing at you, because when they laugh at you they're laughing at me.

And I don't want you cranking any more . . . atoms.

RUTH: *Putting the lipstick back in* BEATRICE's *bag.*
You're almost out of Devil's Kiss.

BEATRICE: If you didn't put so much on it would last longer.

RUTH: Who was that calling?

BEATRICE: Matilda turned me in to the Gestapo.

RUTH: Can I earn a cigarette this morning?

BEATRICE: Why not?

BEATRICE *offers her the backscratcher along with a cigarette.*

RUTH: Was it Mr. Goodman?

BEATRICE: Who?

RUTH: *Lighting the cigarette.*

The call this morning. Was it Mr. Goodman?

BEATRICE: Yes.

RUTH: *Using the backscratcher on* BEATRICE, *who squirms with ecstasy.*
I figured it would be.

BEATRICE: A little higher, please.

RUTH: There?

BEATRICE: Yes, *there* . . . Why did you figure it would be Mr. Goodman?

RUTH: Well, he called me out of sewing class yesterday—I remember because my blouse wasn't all buttoned—and he wanted to know why Tillie's out of school so much.

BEATRICE: Lower. A little lower . . . And what did you tell him?

RUTH: I wish you'd go back to Kools. I liked Kools better.

TILLIE: *Gravely concerned.*
What did you tell him?

RUTH: I told him you were ill, and he
wanted to know what kind, so I told
him you had leprosy.

TILLIE: You didn't!

RUTH: You should have seen his face. He
was so cute. And I told him you had
ringworm and gangrene.

BEATRICE: What did he say?

RUTH: And I told him you had what
Mother's last patient had . . .
whatchamacallit?

BEATRICE: Psoriasis?

RUTH: Yeah. Something like that.

TILLIE: Tell me you didn't, Ruth!

RUTH: O.K. I didn't . . . But I really did.

BEATRICE: He knew you were joking.

RUTH: And then I told him to go look up the *history* and then he'd find out. Whenever they go look up the history then they don't bother me anymore 'cause they think I'm crazy.

BEATRICE: Ruth—

RUTH: And I told him the disease you had was fatal and that there wasn't much hope for you.

BEATRICE: What kind of *history* is it?

RUTH: Just a little folder with the story of our lives in it, that's all.

BEATRICE: How did you ever see it?

RUTH: I read the whole thing last term when Miss Hanley dragged me into the record room because I didn't want to climb the ropes in gym and I told her my skull was growing.

BEATRICE: A little *lower*, please.

RUTH: Lower! Higher! I wish you'd make up your mind. If you'd switch back to Kools it might be worth it, but ugh! these are awful. You know, I really did think my skull was growing. Either that or a tumor. So she dragged me out of gym class, and she thought I couldn't read upside down while she was sitting opposite me with the history. But I could.

BEATRICE: What does it say?

RUTH: Oh, it says you're divorced and that I went crazy . . . and my father took a heart attack at Star Lake . . . and now you're a widow—

BEATRICE: *Referring to the backscratching.* That's it! Hold it right there! Aaah!

RUTH: And it says that I exaggerate and tell stories and that I'm afraid of death and have nightmares . . . and all that stuff.

BEATRICE: And what else does it say?

RUTH: I can't remember everything you know. Remember this, remember that . . . remember this, that . . .

Go to dark. Music in.

TILLIE'S VOICE: Today I saw it. Behind the glass a white cloud began to form. He placed a small piece of metal in the center of the chamber and we waited until I saw the first one—a trace of smoke that came from nowhere and then disappeared. And then another . . . and another, until I knew it was coming from the metal. They looked like water-sprays from a park fountain, and they went on and on for as long as I watched.

And he told me the fountain of smoke would come forth for a long time, and if I had wanted to, I could have stayed there all my life and it would never have ended—that fountain, so close I could have touched it. In front of my eyes, one part of the world was becoming another. Atoms exploding, flinging off tiny bullets that caused the fountain, atom after atom breaking down into something new. And no one could stop the fountain. It would go on for millions of years—on and on, this fountain from eternity.

By the end of this speech, the lights are in to show TILLIE *preparing boxes of dirt in which to plant seeds. The rabbit is in the cage near her, and* BEATRICE *is reading a newspaper on the other side of the room. She is sipping coffee from a huge coffee cup.*

BEATRICE: I thought we had everything, but leave it to you to think of the one thing we're missing . . .

She reads from the newspaper.

Twenty-two acres in Prince's Bay.
Small pond. $6,000 . . . That's
cheap. I'd take a look at it if I had
any money . . .

What kind of seeds are they?

TILLIE: Marigolds. *They've been exposed to cobalt-60.*

BEATRICE: If there's one thing I've always
wanted, it's been a living room
planted with marigolds that have
been exposed to cobalt-60. While
you're at it, why don't you throw in
a tomato patch in the bathroom?

TILLIE: Just let me keep them here for a
week or so until they get started and
then I'll transplant them to the backyard.

BEATRICE: *Reading again.*
Four-family house. Six and a half
and six and a half over five and five.

Eight garages. I could really do something with that. A nursing home . . .

Don't think I'm not kicking myself that I didn't finish that real estate course. I should have finished beauty school, too . . .

God, what I could do with eight garages . . .

There is a sound from beyond the curtained doorway. BEATRICE *gestures in that direction.*

You know, I'm thinking of getting rid of *that* and making this place into something.

TILLIE: Yes.

BEATRICE: I've been thinking about a tea shop. Have you noticed there aren't many of them around anymore?

TILLIE: Yes.

BEATRICE: And this is just the type of neighborhood where a good tea shop could make a go of it. We'd have a good cheesecake. You've got to have a good cheesecake . . .

She calculates.

Eight times ten—well, eight times eight, if they're falling down—that's sixty-four dollars a month from the garages alone . . . I swear money makes money.

There is a rustling at the curtains. Two thin and wrinkled hands push the curtains apart slowly and then the ancient face of NANNY *appears. She negotiates her way through the curtains. She is utterly wrinkled and dried, perhaps a century old. Time has left her with a whisper of a smile —a smile from a soul half-departed. If one looked closely, great cataracts could be seen on each eye, and it is certain that all that can pierce her*

*soundless prison are mere shadows
from the outside world. She pervades
the room with age.*

NANNY *supports herself by a four-
legged tubular frame which she
pushes along in front of her with a
shuffling motion that reminds one of
a ticking clock. Inch by inch she advances into the room.* TILLIE *and*
BEATRICE *continue speaking, knowing that it will be minutes before she
is close enough to know they are
there.*

BEATRICE: What is cobalt-60?

TILLIE: It's something that causes . . .
changes in seeds. Oh, Mother—he
set the cloud chamber up just for
me and he told me about radioactivity and half-life and he got the
seeds for me.

BEATRICE: *Her attention still on the newspaper.*
What does half-life mean?

NANNY *is well into the room as* TIL-
LIE *replies.*

TILLIE: *Reciting from memory.*
The half-life of Polonium-210 is one
hundred and forty days.

The half-life of Radium-226 is one
thousand five hundred and ninety
years.

The half-life of Uranium-238 is four
and one-half billion years.

BEATRICE: *Putting away her newspaper.*
Do you know you're giving me a
headache?

*Then, in a loud, horribly saccharine
voice, she speaks to* NANNY *as if she
were addressing a deaf year-old
child.*

LOOK WHO'S THERE! IT'S
NANNY! NANNY CAME ALL
THE WAY OUT HERE BY HER-
SELF!

I'm going to need a cigarette for this.

NANNY! YOU COME SIT DOWN AND WE'LL BE RIGHT WITH HER!

You know, sometimes I've got to laugh. I've got *this* on my hands and all you're worried about is planting marigolds.

I'VE GOT HOTSY WATER FOR YOU, NANNY. WOULD YOU LIKE SOME HOTSY WATER AND HONEY?

NANNY *has seated herself at a table, smiling but oblivious to her environment.*

I've never seen it to fail. Every time I decide to have a cup of coffee I see that face at the curtains. I wonder what she'd do . . .

She holds pot of boiling water.

. . . if I just poured this right over her head. I'll bet she wouldn't even notice it.

NANNY'S GOING TO GET JUST WHAT SHE NEEDS!

She fills a cup for her and places a honey jar near her.

You know if someone told me when I was young that I'd end up feeding honey to a zombie, I'd tell them they were crazy.

SOMETHING WRONG, NANNY? OH, DID I FORGET NANNY'S SPOON? MERCY! MERCY! I FORGOT NANNY'S SPOON!

She gets a spoon and stands behind NANNY.

I'll give you a spoon, Nanny, I'll give you a spoon.

She makes a motion behind NANNY's
*back as if she's going to smack her
on the head with the spoon.*

Matilda! Watch me give Nanny her
spoon.

A SPOON FOR NANNY!

It manages to be slightly funny and
TILLIE *yields to a laugh, along with
her mother.*

Fifty dollars a week. Fifty dollars.
I look at you, Nanny, and I wonder
if it's worth it. I think I'd be better
off driving a cab.

TAKE HONEY, NANNY. HONEY
WITH HOTSY WATER!

You should have seen her daughter
bring her here last week . . . I
could have used you that day . . .
She came in pretending she was Miss
Career Woman of the Year. She said

she was in real estate and *such a busy little woman,* such a busy little woman—she just couldn't give all the love and care and affection her little momsy needed anymore . . .

Then, with a great smile, she speaks right into NANNY's *uncomprehending face.*

Nanny's quite a little cross to bear, now aren't you, Nanny dear? But you're a little better than Mr. Mayo was—with the tumor on his brain— or Miss Marion Minto with her cancer, or Mr. Brougham . . . what was his first name?

TILLIE: Alexander.

BEATRICE: Mr. Alexander Brougham with the worms in his legs.

WHY, NANNY'S QUITE SOME LITTLE GIRL, AREN'T YOU, NANNY? A GIRL DRINKING HER HOTSY AND HONEY! . . .

Cobalt-60. Ha! You take me for a fool, don't you?

TILLIE: No, Mother.

BEATRICE: Science, science, science! Don't they teach our misfits anything anymore? Anything decent and meaningful and sensitive? Do you know what I'd be now if it wasn't for this mud pool I got sucked into? I'd probably be a dancer. Miss Betty Frank, The Best Dancer of the Class of 19 . . . something. One minute I'm the best dancer in school—smart as a whip— the head of the whole crowd! And the next minute . . .

One mistake. That's how it starts. Marry the wrong man and before you know it he's got you tied down with two stones around your neck for the rest of your life.

When I was in that lousy high school I was one of the most respected kids you ever saw.

I used to wonder why people always said, "Why, just yesterday . . . why, just yesterday . . . why, just yesterday . . ."

Before I knew what happened I lost my dancing legs and got varicose legs. Beautiful varicose legs. Do you know, everything I ever thought I'd be has exploded!

NANNY, YOU HURRY UP WITH THAT HONEY!

Exploded! You know, I almost forgot about everything I was supposed to be . . .

NANNY'S ALMOST FINISHED. ISN'T THAT WONDERFUL?

She's almost finished, all right.

NANNY'S DAUGHTER IS COMING TO SEE YOU SOON. WILL THAT MAKE NANNY HAPPY?

The day Miss Career Woman of the Year comes to visit again I think I'll drop dead. Nobody's too busy for anything they want to do, don't you tell me. What kind of an idiot do people take me for?

NANNY, YOU'RE SPILLING YOUR HOTSY! JESUS CHRIST!

You know, I ought to kick you right out and open that tea shop tomorrow.

Oh, it's coming. I can feel it. And the first thing I'll do is get rid of that rabbit.

TILLIE: *Hardly listening.*
Yes, Mother.

BEATRICE: You think I'm kidding?

TILLIE: No, I don't.

BEATRICE: You bet I'm not!

She rummages through some drawers in a chest.

I was going to do this a month ago.

She holds up a small bottle.

Here it is. Here's a new word for you.

She reads.

Trichloro . . . methane. Do you know what that is, Matilda? Well, it's chloroform!

She puts the bottle away.

I'm saving it for that Angora manure machine of yours. Speaking of manure machines, IS NANNY READY TO GO MAKE DUTY?

She starts helping NANNY *out of the chair and props her up with the tubular frame.*

NANNY IS ALWAYS READY FOR DUTY, AREN'T YOU NANNY?

BECAUSE NANNY'S A GOODY-GOODY GIRL AND GOODY-GOODY GIRLS ALWAYS GET GOODY-GOODY THINGS. GOD LOOKS OUT FOR GOODY-GOODY GIRLS AND GIVES THEM HOTSY AND HONEY— RIGHT, NANNY?

BEATRICE *sits down in the hall and watches* NANNY *make her way toward the bathroom. There is a pause as the woman's shuffling continues.*

The lights go low on TILLIE, NANNY *becomes a silhouette, and the light remains on* BEATRICE. *She starts to read the paper again, but the shuffling gets on her nerves and she flings the paper down.*

Half-life! If you want to know what a half-life is, just ask me. You're looking at the original half-life!

I got stuck with one daughter with half a mind; another one who's half a test tube; half a husband—a house half full of rabbit crap—and half a corpse!

That's what I call a half-life, Matilda! Me and cobalt-60! Two of the biggest half-*lifes* you ever saw!

The set goes to dark.

After a few seconds, the sound of someone dialing a phone can be heard. As the spot comes up on her, we see BEATRICE *holding the phone and struggling to get a cigarette.*

BEATRICE: *On the phone.*
Hello—Mr. Goodman, please . . . How would I know if he's got a class? . . . Hello, Mr. Goodman? Are you Mr. Goodman? . . . Oh, I beg your pardon, Miss Torgersen . . . Yes, I'll wait . . .

She lights her cigarette.

Couldn't you find him, Miss Torgersen? . . . Oh! Excuse me, Mr. Goodman. How are you? . . . I'll bet you'll never guess who this is—it's Mrs. Hunsdorfer—remember the frozen foods?

She laughs.

You know, Ruth told me she's your new secretary and I certainly think that's a delight. You were paying so much attention to Matilda that I'll bet Ruth just got jealous. She does things like that, you know. I hope she works hard for you, although I can't imagine what kind of work Ruth could be doing in that great big science office. She's a terrible snoop . . .

She takes a puff.

Your attendance? Isn't that charming. And the *cut* cards! Imagine. You trust her with . . . why, I didn't know she could type *at all*

. . . imagine. Well . . . I'll . . . Of course, *too* much work isn't good for anyone, either. No wonder she's failing everything. I mean, I never knew a girl who failed everything regardless of what they were suffering from. I suppose I should say *recovering* from . . .

Well, it's about the seeds you gave Matilda . . . Well, she's had them in the house for a week now and they're starting to grow. Now, she told me they had been subjected to radioactivity, and I hear such terrible things about radioactivity that I automatically associate radioactivity with sterility, and it positively horrifies me to have those seeds right here in my living room. Couldn't she just grow plain marigolds like everyone else?

She takes a puff.

Oh . . .

*Another big puff, forming a mush-
room cloud.*

It does sound like an interesting
project, but . . .

The biggest puff yet.

No, I must admit that at this very
moment I don't know what a *muta-
tion* is . . .

She laughs uncomfortably.

Mr. Goodman . . . Mr. Goodman! I
don't want you to think I'm not inter-
ested, but please spare me definitions
over the phone. I'll go to the library
next week and pick me out some
little book on science and then I'll
know all about mutations . . . No,
you didn't insult me, but I just want
you to know that I'm not *stupid* . . .

I just thought prevention was better
than a tragedy, Mr. Goodman. I

mean, Matilda has enough problems to worry about without *sterility* . . .

Well, I was just concerned, but you've put my poor mother's heart at ease. You know, really, our schools need more exciting young men like you, I really mean that. Really. Oh, I do. Goodbye, Mr. Goodman.

By the end of her talk on the phone, her face is left in a spotlight, and then the stage goes black. The music theme comes in, in a minor key, softly at first, but accentuated by increasingly loud pulses which transmute into thunder crashes.

There is a scream heard from upstairs and we see the set in night shadows.

TILLIE *tears open her bedroom door and rushes into* BEATRICE'S *room.* RUTH *screams again.*

TILLIE: Mother! She's going to have one!

*RUTH appears on the landing and re-
leases another scream which breaks
off into gasps. She starts down the
stairs and stops halfway to scream
again. There is another tremendous
thunder crash as* BEATRICE *comes out
of her room, puts on the hall light,
and catches the hysterical girl on the
stairs.*

BEATRICE: *Shouting.*
Stop it! Stop it, Ruth!

TILLIE: *At the top of the stairs.*
She's going!

BEATRICE: Ruth! Stop it!

TILLIE: She's going to go!

BEATRICE: *Yelling at* TILLIE.
Shut up and get back in your room!

Ruth screams.

You're not going to let yourself go,
do you hear me, Ruth? You're not
going to go!

RUTH: He's after me!

*She screams, lightning and thunder
crash follow.*

BEATRICE: You were dreaming, do you hear me?
Nobody's after you! Nobody!

TILLIE: I saw her eyes start to go back—

BEATRICE: *To* TILLIE.
Get back in your room!

She helps RUTH *down the rest of the
stairs.*

There, now, nobody's after you. Nice
and easy. Breathe deeply . . . Did
the big bad man come after my little
girl?

She sits RUTH *down and then puts
both hands up to her own face and*

pulls her features into a comic mask.
RUTH *begins to laugh at her.*

That big bad bogey man?

They both laugh heartily.

Now that wasn't so bad, was it?

RUTH: It was the dream, with Mr. Mayo again.

BEATRICE: Oh. Well, we'll just get you a little hot milk and—

A tremendous thunder crash throws the set into shadows.

Why, the electricity's gone off. Do you remember what happened to those candles?

RUTH: What candles?

BEATRICE: The little white ones from my birthday cake last year.

RUTH: Tillie melted them down for school a long time ago.

BEATRICE: *Searching through drawers.*
She had no right doing that.

RUTH: She asked you. She used them to attach a paper straw to a milk bottle with a balloon over it, and it was supposed to tell if it was going to rain.

BEATRICE: *Finding a flashlight.*
There! It works. I don't want her wasting anything of mine unless she's positive I won't need it. You always need candles.

She steers Ruth toward the couch as lightning flashes.

Why, Ruth—your skin just turned ice cold!

She rummages through one of the boxes and grabs a blanket.

This will warm you up . . . What's
the matter?

RUTH: The flashlight—

BEATRICE: What's wrong with it?

RUTH: It's the same one I used to check on
Mr. Mayo with.

BEATRICE: So it is. We don't need it.

RUTH: No, let me keep it.

Starting to laugh.

Do you want to know how they have
it in the history?

BEATRICE: No, I don't.

RUTH: Well, they say I came out of my
room . . .

She flashes the light on her room.

. . . And I started down the stairs,
step by step . . . and I heard the

choking and banging on the bed, and . . .

BEATRICE: I'm going back to bed.

RUTH: No!

BEATRICE: Well, talk about something nice, then.

RUTH: Oh, Mama, tell me about the wagon.

BEATRICE: You change so fast I can't keep up with you.

RUTH: Mama, *please* . . . the story about the wagon.

BEATRICE: I don't know anything about telling stories. Get those great big smart teachers of yours to do that sort of stuff.

RUTH: Tell me about the horses again, and how you stole the wagon.

BEATRICE: Don't get me started on that.

RUTH: Mama, *please* . . .

BEATRICE: *Taking out a pack of cigarettes.*
Do you want a cigarette?

RUTH: *Taking one.*
Leave out the part where they shoot the horses, though.

They both light up.

BEATRICE: Honey, you know the whole story—

RUTH: "Apples! Pears! *Cu* . . . cumbers!"

BEATRICE: No. It's "Apples! Pears! Cu*cum* . . . bers!"

They say it together.

"Apples! Pears! Cu*cum* . . . bers!"

And they laugh.

RUTH: How did you get the wagon out without him seeing you?

BEATRICE: That was easy. Every time he got home for the day he'd make us both some sandwiches—my mama had been dead for years—and he'd take a nap on the old sofa that used to be . . . there!

She points to a corner of the room.

And while he was sleeping I got the horses hitched up and went riding around the block waving to everyone.

RUTH: Oh, Mama, you didn't!

BEATRICE: Of course I did. I had more nerve than a bear when I was a kid. Let me tell you it takes nerve to sit up on that wagon every day yelling "Apples! . . .

Both together.

Pears! Cu*cum* . . . bers!"

They laugh again.

RUTH: Did he find out you took the wagon?

BEATRICE: Did he find out? He came running down the street after me and started spanking me right on top of the wagon—not hard—but it was so embarrassing—and I had one of those penny marshmallow ships in the back pocket of my overalls, and it got all squished. And you better believe I never did it again . . .

You would have loved him, Ruth, and gone out with him on the wagon . . . all over Stapleton yelling as loud as you wanted.

RUTH: "Apples! Pears! *Cu* . . . cumbers!"

BEATRICE: No!

RUTH: "Cu*cum* . . . bers!"

BEATRICE: My father made up for all the other men in this whole world, Ruth. If only you two could have met. He'd only be about seventy now, do you realize that? And I'll bet he'd still be selling vegetables around town. All that fun—and then I don't think I ever knew what really hit me.

RUTH: Don't tell about—

BEATRICE: Don't worry about the horses.

RUTH: What hit you?

BEATRICE: Well it was just me and Papa . . . and your father hanging around. And then Papa got sick . . . and I drove with him up to the sanatorium. And then I came home and there were the horses—

RUTH: Mother!

BEATRICE: And I had the horses . . . taken care of. And then Papa got terribly sick and he begged me to marry so that he'd be sure I'd be taken care of.

She laughs.

If he knew how I was taken care of
he'd turn over in his grave.

And *nightmares!* Do you want to
know the nightmare I used to have?

I never had nightmares over the
fights with your father, or the di-
vorce, or his thrombosis—he de-
served it—I never had nightmares
over any of that.

Let me tell you about my nightmare
that used to come back and back:

Well, I'm on Papa's wagon, but it's
newer and shinier, and it's being
pulled by beautiful white horses,
not dirty workhorses—these are like
circus horses with long manes and
tinsel—and the wagon is blue, shiny
blue. And it's full—filled with yel-
low apples and grapes and green
squash.

You're going to laugh when you hear this. I'm wearing a lovely gown with jewels all over it, and my hair is piled up on top of my head with a long feather in it, and the bells are ringing.

Huge bells swinging on a gold braid strung across the back of the wagon, and they're going DONG, DONG . . . DONG, DONG. And I'm yelling "APPLES! PEARS! CUCUM . . . BERS!"

RUTH: That doesn't sound like a nightmare to me.

BEATRICE: And then I turn down our street and all the noise stops. This long street, with all the doors of the houses shut and everything crowded next to each other, and there's not a soul around. And then I start getting afraid that the vegetables are going to spoil . . . and that nobody's going to buy anything, and I feel as though I shouldn't be on the wagon, and I keep trying to call out.

But there isn't a sound. Not a single sound. Then I turn my head and look at the house across the street. I see an upstairs window, and a pair of hands pull the curtains slowly apart. I see the face of my father and my heart stands still . . .

Ruth . . . take the light out of my eyes.

A long pause.

RUTH: Is Nanny going to die here?

BEATRICE: No.

RUTH: How can you be sure?

BEATRICE: I can tell.

RUTH: Are you crying?

BEATRICE: What's left for me, Ruth?

RUTH: What, Mama?

BEATRICE: What's left for me?

The stage goes slowly to dark as the drizzling rain becomes louder and then disappears.

When the lights come up again NANNY *is seated at the kitchen table with a bottle of beer and a glass in front of her.* TILLIE *comes in the front door with a box of large marigold plants and sets them down where they'll be inconspicuous. She gets the rabbit out of its cage, sits down near* NANNY *and gives her a little wave.* BEATRICE *suddenly appears at the top of the stairs and drops a stack of newspapers with a loud thud. She goes back into her room and lets fly another armful of junk.*

TILLIE: What are you doing?

BEATRICE: A little housecleaning, and you're going to help. You can start by getting rid of that rabbit or I'll suffocate the bastard.

She takes a drink from a glass of whiskey.

You don't think I will, do you? You wait and see. Where's Ruth? She's probably running around the schoolyard in her brassiere.

She comes downstairs.

TILLIE: Mother, they want me to do something at school.

BEATRICE: NANNY! DID YOU HEAR THAT? THEY WANT HER TO DO SOMETHING AT SCHOOL! ISN'T THAT MOMENTOUS, NANNY?

Well I want you to do something around here. Like get rid of that bunny. I'm being generous! I'll let you give it away. Far away. Give it to Mr. Goodman. I'd chloroform the thing myself, but that crazy sister of yours would throw convulsions for fifty years . . . and I hate a house that vibrates.

And get rid of those sterile marigolds. They stink!

HI, NANNY—HOW ARE YOU, HONEY? HOW WOULD YOU LIKE TO GO ON A LONG TRIP?

You see, everybody, I spent today taking stock of my life and I've come up with zero. I added up all the separate departments and the total reads zero . . .

zero zero zero zero zero zero zero zero zero zero zero zero

zero zero zero
zero zero
zero

. . . And do you know how you
pronounce that, with all your gram-
matical schoolin' and foolin'? You
pronounce it o,o,o,o,O,O,O,O,O,O!
o,o,o,o,O,O,O,O,O,O,O,O!

Right, Nanny? RIGHT, NANNY?

 So, by the end of the week, you get
rid of that cottontail compost heap
and we'll get you a job down at the
five-and-ten-cent store. And if you
don't do so well with the public,
we'll fix you up with some kind of
machine. Wouldn't that be nice?

*Ruth enters at a gallop, throwing her
books down and babbling a mile a
minute.*

RUTH: *Enthusiastically.*
Can you believe it? I didn't, until

Chris Burns came up and told me about it in Geography, and then Mr. Goodman told me himself during the eighth period in the office when I was eavesdropping. Aren't you so happy you could bust? Tillie? I'm so proud I can't believe it, Mama. Everybody was talking about it and nobody . . . well, it was the first time they all came up screaming about her and I said, "Yes, she's my sister!" I said it, "She's my sister! My sister! My *sister!*" Give me a cigarette.

BEATRICE: Get your hands off my personal property.

RUTH: I'll scratch your back later.

BEATRICE: I don't want you to touch me!

RUTH: Did he call yet? My God, I can't believe it, I just can't!

BEATRICE: Did who call yet?

RUTH: I'm not supposed to tell you, as Mr. Goodman's private secretary, but you're going to get a call from school.

BEATRICE: *To* TILLIE.
What is she talking about?

TILLIE: I was in the Science Fair at school.

RUTH: Didn't she tell you yet? Oh, Tillie, how could you? She's fantastic, Mama! She's a finalist in the Science Fair. There were only five of them out of hundreds and hundreds. She won with all those plants over there. They're freaks! Isn't that a scream? Dr. Berg picked her himself. The principal! And I heard Mr. Goodman say she was going to be another Madam Pasteur and he never saw a girl do anything like that before and . . . so I told everybody, "Yes, she's my sister!" Tillie, "You're my sister!" I said. And Mr. Goodman called the Advance and they're coming to take your picture. Oh, Mama, isn't it crazy? And nobody laughed at her, Mama. She beat out practically everybody and nobody laughed at her. "She's my sister," I said. "She's my sister!"

The telephone rings.

That must be him! Mama, answer it —I'm afraid.

Ring.

Answer it before he hangs up!

Ring.

Mama! He's gonna hang up!

Ruth grabs the phone.

Hello? . . . Yes . . .

Aside to BEATRICE.

It's him! . . . Just a minute, please . . .

Covering the mouthpiece.

He wants to talk to you.

BEATRICE: Who?

RUTH: The *principal!*

BEATRICE: Hang up.

RUTH: I told him you were here! Mama!

BEATRICE *gets up and shuffles slowly to the phone.*

BEATRICE: *Finally, into the phone.*
Yes? . . . I know who you are, Dr. Berg . . . I see . . . Couldn't you get someone else? There's an awfully lot of work that has to be done around here, because she's not as careful with her home duties as she is with man-in-the-moon marigolds . . .

Me? What would you want with me

up on the stage? . . . The other mothers can do as they please . . . I would have thought you had enough in your *history* without . . . I'll think about it . . . Goodbye, Dr. Berg . . .

Pause, then screaming.

I SAID I'D THINK ABOUT IT!

She hangs up the phone, turns her face slowly to RUTH, *then to* TILLIE, *who has her face hidden in shame in the rabbit's fur.*

RUTH: What did he say?

BEATRICE: *Flinging her glass on the floor.*
How could you do this to me? HOW COULD YOU LET THAT MAN CALL OUR HOME!

I have no clothes, do you hear me? I'd look just like you up on the stage, ugly little you!

DO YOU WANT THEM TO
LAUGH AT US? LAUGH AT
THE TWO OF US?

RUTH: *Disbelievingly.*
Mother . . . aren't you proud of
her? Mother . . . it's an *honor.*

TILLIE *breaks into tears and moves
away from* BEATRICE. *It seems as
though she is crushed, but then she
halts and turns to face her mother.*

TILLIE: *Through tears.*
But . . . nobody laughed at me.

BEATRICE's *face begins to soften as
she glimpses what she's done to*
TILLIE.

BEATRICE: Oh, my God . . .

TILLIE *starts toward her.* BEATRICE
*opens her arms to receive her as mu-
sic starts in and lights fade. A chord
of finality punctuates the end of
Act I.*

67

DONG KINGMAN

ACT II

About two weeks later.

The room looks somewhat cheery and there is excitement in the air. It is early evening and preparations are being made for TILLIE *to take her project to the final judging of the Science Fair.*

TILLIE *has been dressed by her mother in clothes which are clean but too girlish for her awkwardness. Her hair has been curled, she sports a large bow, and her dress is a starched flair.*

RUTH *has dressed herself up as well. She has put on too much makeup, and her lipstick has been extended beyond the natural line of her lips. She almost appears to be sinister.*

A large three-panel screen stands on one of the tables. THE EFFECT OF GAMMA RAYS ON MAN-IN-THE-MOON MARIGOLDS is printed in large letters running across the top of the three panels. Below this on each panel there is a subtopic: THE PAST; THE PRESENT; THE FUTURE. *Additional charts and data appear below the titles.*

RUTH: The only competition you have to worry about is Janice Vickery. They say she caught it near Princess Bay Boulevard and it was still alive when she took the skin off it.

TILLIE: *Taking some plants from* RUTH.
Let me do that, please, Ruth.

RUTH: I'm sorry I touched them, really.

TILLIE: Why don't you feed Peter?

RUTH: Because I don't feel like feeding him . . . Now I feel like feeding him.

She gets some lettuce from a bag.

I heard that it screamed for three minutes after she put it in because the water wasn't boiling yet. How much talent does it take to boil the skin off a cat and then stick the bones together again? That's what I want to know. Ugh. I had a dream about that, too. I figure she did it in less than a day and she ends up as one of the top five winners . . . and you spend months growing atomic flowers.

TILLIE: Don't you think you should finish getting ready?

RUTH: Finish? This is it!

TILLIE: Are you going to wear that sweater?

RUTH: Look, don't worry about me. I'm not getting up on any stage, and if I did I wouldn't be caught dead with a horrible bow like that.

TILLIE: Mother put it—

RUTH: They're going to laugh you off the stage again like when you cranked that atom in assembly . . . I didn't mean that . . . The one they're going to laugh at is Mama.

TILLIE: What?

RUTH: I said the one they're going to laugh at is Mama . . . Oh, let me take that bow off.

TILLIE: It's all right.

RUTH: Look, just sit still. I don't want everybody making fun of you.

TILLIE: What made you say that about Mama?

RUTH: Oh, I heard them talking in the Science Office yesterday. Mr. Goodman and Miss Hanley. She's getting $12.63 to chaperon the thing tonight.

TILLIE: What were they saying?

RUTH: Miss Hanley was telling Mr. Goodman about Mama . . . when she found out you were one of the five winners. And he wanted to know if there was something wrong with Mama because she sounded crazy over the phone. And Miss Hanley said she *was* crazy and she always has been crazy and she can't wait to see what she looks like after all these years. Miss Hanley said her nickname used to be *Betty the Loon.*

TILLIE: *As* RUTH *combs her hair.*
Ruth, you're hurting me.

RUTH: She was just like you and everybody thought she was a big weirdo. There! You look much better!

She goes back to the rabbit.

Peter, if anybody stuck you in a pot of boiling water I'd kill them, do you know that? . . .

Then to TILLIE.

What do they call boiling the skin off a cat? I call it murder, that's what I call it. They say it was hit by a car and Janice just scooped it up and before you could say *bingo* it was screaming in a pot of boiling water . . .

Do you know what they're all waiting to see? Mama's feathers! That's what Miss Hanley said. She said Mama blabs as though she was the Queen of England and just as proper as can be, and that her idea of getting dressed up is to put on all the feathers in the world and go as a bird. Always trying to get somewhere, like a great big bird.

TILLIE: Don't tell Mama, please. It doesn't matter.

RUTH: I was up there watching her getting dressed and sure enough, she's got the feathers out.

TILLIE: You didn't tell her what Miss Hanley said?

RUTH: Are you kidding? I just told her I didn't like the feathers and I didn't think she should wear any. But I'll bet she doesn't listen to me.

TILLIE: It doesn't matter.

RUTH: It doesn't matter? Do you think I want to be laughed right out of the school tonight, with Chris Burns there, and all? Laughed right out of the school, with your electric hair and her feathers on that stage, and Miss Hanley splitting her sides?

TILLIE: Promise me you won't say anything.

RUTH: On one condition.

TILLIE: What?

RUTH: Give Peter to me.

TILLIE: *Ignoring her.*
The taxi will be here any minute and I won't have all this stuff ready. Did you see my speech?

RUTH: I mean it. Give Peter to me.

TILLIE: He belongs to all of us.

RUTH: For me. All for me. What do you care? He doesn't mean anything to you anymore, now that you've got all those crazy plants.

TILLIE: Will you stop?

RUTH: If you don't give him to me I'm going to tell Mama that everybody's waiting to laugh at her.

TILLIE: Where are those typewritten cards?

RUTH: I MEAN IT! Give him to me!

TILLIE: Does he mean that much to you?

RUTH: Yes!

TILLIE: All right.

RUTH: *After a burst of private laughter.*
Betty the Loon . . .

She laughs again.

That's what they used to call her,
you know. Betty the Loon!

TILLIE: I don't think that's very nice.

RUTH: First they had Betty the Loon, and
now they've got Tillie the Loon . . .

To rabbit.

You don't have to worry about
me turning you in for any old
plants . . .

How much does a taxi cost from here
to the school?

TILLIE: Not much.

RUTH: I wish she'd give me the money it costs for a taxi—and for all that cardboard and paint and flowerpots and stuff. The only time she ever made a fuss over me was when she drove me nuts.

TILLIE: Tell her to hurry, please.

RUTH: By the way, I went over to see Janice Vickery's pot, that she did you know what in, and I started telling her and her mother about the worms in Mr. Alexander Brougham's legs, and I got thrown out because it was too near dinner time. That Mrs. Vickery kills me. She can't stand worms in somebody else's legs but she lets her daughter cook a cat.

TILLIE: *Calling upstairs.*
Mother! The taxi will be here any minute.

BEATRICE *comes to the top of the stairs. Her costume is strange, but not that strange, by any means. She is even a little attractive tonight, and though her words say she is greatly annoyed with having to attend the night's function, her tone and direction show she is very, very proud.*

BEATRICE: You're lucky I'm coming, without all this rushing me.

TILLIE: Mama, you look beautiful.

BEATRICE: Don't put it on too thick. I said I'd go and I guess there's no way to get out of it. Do you mind telling me how I'm supposed to get up on the stage? Do they call my name or what? And where are you going to be? If you ask me, they should've sent all the parents a mimeographed sheet of instructions. If this is supposed to be such a great event, why don't they do it right?

TILLIE: You just sit on the stage with the other parents before it begins.

BEATRICE: How long is this thing going to last? And remember, I don't care even if you do win the whole damn thing, I'm not making any speech. I can hold my own anywhere, but I hated that school when I went there and I hate it now . . . and the only thing I'd have to say is, what a pack of stupid teachers and vicious children they have. Imagine someone tearing the skin off a cat.

RUTH: She didn't tear it. She boiled it off.

BEATRICE: You just told me upstairs that girl tore the skin off with an orange knife and . . . do you know, sometimes you exasperate me?

To TILLIE.

If you've got all the plants in this box, I can manage the folding thing. Do you know I've got a headache from doing those titles? And you probably don't even like them.

TILLIE: I like them very much.

BEATRICE: Look, if you don't want me to go tonight, I don't have to. You're about as enthusiastic as a dummy about this whole thing.

TILLIE: I'm sorry.

BEATRICE: And I refuse to let you get nervous. Put that bow back in your hair.

RUTH: I took it out.

BEATRICE: What did you do that for?

RUTH: *Taking the rabbit in her arms.* Because it made her look crazy.

BEATRICE: How would you know what's crazy or not? If that sweater of yours was any tighter it'd cut off the circulation in your chest.

Fussing over TILLIE.

The bow looks very nice in your hair. There's nothing wrong with looking proper, Matilda, and if you don't have enough money to look expensive and perfect, people like you for *trying* to look nice. You know, one day maybe you will be pretty. You'll have some nice features, when that hair revives and you do some tricks with makeup. I hope you didn't crowd the plants too close together. Did you find your speech?

TILLIE: Yes, Mother.

BEATRICE: You know, Matilda, I was wondering about something. Do you think you're really going to win? I mean, not that you won't be the best, but there's so much politics in school. Don't laugh, but if there's anyone who's an expert on that, it's me, and someday I'm going to write a book and blast that school to pieces. If you're just a little bit different in this world, they try to kill you off.

RUTH: *Putting on her coat.*
           Tillie gave Peter to me.

BEATRICE: Oh? Then you inherited the rabbit
           droppings I found upstairs. What
           are you doing with your coat on?

RUTH: I'm going out to wait for the taxi.

BEATRICE: Oh, no you're not. You start right in
           on the rabbit droppings. Or you
           won't get another cigarette even if
           you scratch my back with an orange
           knife.

RUTH: I'm going down to the school with
           you.

BEATRICE: Oh, no you're not! You're going to
           keep company with that corpse in
           there. If she wakes up and starts
           gagging just slip her a shot of whis-
           key.

           The taxi horn blows outside.

Quick! Grab the plants, Matilda—
I'll get the big thing.

RUTH: I want to go! I promised Chris Burns
I'd meet him.

BEATRICE: Can't you understand English?

RUTH: I've got to go!

BEATRICE: Shut up!

RUTH: *Almost berserk.*
I don't care. I'M GOING ANYWAY!

BEATRICE: *Shoving* RUTH *hard.*
WHAT DID YOU SAY?

TILLIE: Mother!

After a pause, the horn blows again.

BEATRICE: Hurry up with that box, Matilda, and
tell him to stop blowing the horn.
HURRY UP!

TILLIE *reluctantly exits with the box of plants.*

I don't know where you ever got the idea you were going tonight. Did you think nobody was going to hold down the fort? . . .

Now you know how I felt all those years you and everybody else was running out whenever they felt like it—because there was always me to watch over the fifty-dollar-a-week corpse. If there's one thing I demand it's respect. I don't ask for anything from you but respect.

RUTH: *Pathetically.*
Why are you ashamed of me?

BEATRICE: I've been seen with a lot worse than you. I don't even know why I'm going tonight, do you know that? Do you think I give one goddam about the whole thing? . . .

She starts to fold the large three-panel screen with the titles: THE PAST, THE PRESENT, *and* THE FUTURE.

Do you want to know why I'm going? Do you really want to know why this once somebody else has to stick with that dried prune for a few minutes? Because this is the first time in my life I've ever felt just a little bit proud over something. Isn't that silly? Somewhere in the back of this turtle-sized brain of mine I feel just a little *proud!* Jesus Christ! And you begrudge me even that, you little bastard.

The taxi horn blows impatiently.

RUTH: *In a hard voice.*
Hurry up. They're waiting for you . . . They're *all* waiting for you.

BEATRICE: *Carrying the folded screen so that* THE PAST *is face out in bold black letters.*

I hope the paint is dry . . . Who's waiting for me?

RUTH: Everybody . . . including Miss Hanley. She's been telling all the teachers . . . about you . . . and they're all waiting.

BEATRICE: You're such a little liar, Ruth, do you know that? When you can't have what you want, you try to ruin it for everybody else.

She starts to the door.

RUTH: Goodnight, *Betty the Loon.*

BEATRICE *stops as if she's been stabbed.*

The taxi horn blows several times as BEATRICE *puts down the folding screen.*

BEATRICE: *Helplessly.*
Take this thing.

RUTH: What for?

BEATRICE: Go with Matilda.

RUTH: I don't want to go now.

BEATRICE: *Blasting.*
           GET OUT OF HERE!

RUTH: *After a long pause.*
           Now Tillie's going to blame it on
           me that you're not going—and take
           the rabbit back.

           The taxi beeps again, as RUTH *puts
           her coat on.*

           I can't help it what people call you.

           She picks up the screen.

           I'll tell Tillie you'll be down later,
           all right? . . .

           Don't answer me. What do I care!

           RUTH *exits.*

90

BEATRICE *breaks into tears that shudder her body, and the lights go down slowly on her pathetic form. Music in.*

*Suddenly a bolt of light strikes an area in the right stage—*JANICE VICKERY *is standing in the spotlight holding the skeleton of a cat mounted on a small platform. Her face and voice are smug.*

JANICE: *The Past:* I got the cat from the A.S.P.C.A. immediately after it had been killed by a high-altitude pressure system. That explains why some of the rib bones are missing, because that method sucks the air out of the animal's lungs and ruptures all cavities. They say it prevents cruelty to animals but I think it's horrible.

She laughs.

Then I boiled the cat in a sodium hydroxide solution until most of the skin pulled right off, but I had to scrape some of the grizzle off the joints with a knife. You have no idea how difficult it is to get right down to the bones.

A little gong sounds.

I have to go on to *The Present,* now —but I did want to tell you how long it took me to put the thing together. I mean, as it is now, it's extremely useful for students of anatomy, even with the missing rib bones, and it can be used to show basic anatomical aspects of many, many animals that are in the same family as felines. I suppose that's about the only present uses I can think for it, but it is nice to remember as an accomplishment, and it looks good on college applications to show you did something else in school besides dating.

She laughs, and a second gong sounds.

The Future: The only future plans I have for Tabby—my little brother asked the A.S.P.C.A. what its name was when he went to pick it up and they said it was called Tabby, but I think they were kidding him—

She laughs again.

I mean as far as future plans, I'm going to donate it to the science department, of course, and next year, if there's another Science Fair perhaps I'll do the same thing with a dog.

A third gong sounds.

Thank you very much for your attention, and I hope I win!

JANICE *and her spotlight disappear as suddenly as they had arrived, and music returns as the lights come up slowly on* BEATRICE.

She has obviously been drinking and is going through a phone book. Find-

ing her number, she goes to the phone and dials.

BEATRICE: *Into the phone.*
I want to talk to the principal, please . . .

Well, you'll have to get him down off the stage . . .

It's none of your goddam business who I am! . . .

Oh, I see . . . Yes. I have a message for him and Mr. Goodman, and you, too . . . And this is for Miss Hanley, too . . .

Tell them Mrs. Hunsdorfer called to thank them for making her wish she was dead . . . Would you give them that message, please? . . . Thank you very much.

She hangs up the phone, pauses, then surveys the room. Her attention fixes on the store window covered with newspapers. The phone rings several times but she ignores it. She goes to the window and proceeds to rip the paper from it. That finished, she turns and surveys the room again. She goes to the kitchen table and rearranges its position. She spies a card table with school supplies and hurls them on the floor. Next, she goes to a bureau and rummages through drawers, finding tablecloths and napkins. She throws cloths on two or three tables and is heading toward the kitchen table when the phone rings again. The ringing triggers off something else she wants to do. She empties a cup filled with scraps of paper and finds a telephone number. She lifts the receiver off the ringing phone and hangs up immediately. She lifts the receiver again, checks to make sure there's a dial tone, and then dials the number on the scrap of paper.

BEATRICE: *Into the phone.*

Hello. This is Mrs. Hunsdorfer . . . I'm sorry if I frightened you, I wouldn't want you to think Nanny had deceased or anything like that —I can imagine how terrible you'd feel if anything like that ever happened . . . Terrible tragedy that would be, Miss Career Woman of the Year . . .

Yes, I'll tell you why I'm calling. I want her out of here by tomorrow. I told you when you rolled her in here I was going to try her out for a while and if I didn't like her she was to get the hell out. Well I don't like her, so get her the hell out . . .

It's like this. I don't like the way she cheats at solitaire. Is that a good enough reason? . . . Fine. And if she's not out of here by noon I'll send her collect in an ambulance, you son of a bitch!

*She slams down the phone and bursts
into laughter. The laughter subsides
somewhat as she pours herself another drink. She takes the drink to
a chair and as she sits down her foot
accidentally hits the rabbit cage. She
gives the cage a little kick and then
an idea strikes. She gets up and finds
a large blue towel which she flings
over her shoulder. She gets the bottle
of chloroform and approaches the
cage. Having reached a decision she
picks up the cage and takes it upstairs.*

Music in and lights fade.

*From the darkness a beam of light
falls on* TILLIE *in the same way* JAN-
ICE VICKERY *had been presented.*

TILLIE: *Deathly afraid, and referring to her
cards.*
The Past: The seeds were exposed
to various degrees . . . of gamma

rays from radiation sources in Oak Ridge . . .

Mr. Goodman helped me pay for the seeds . . . Their growth was plotted against . . . time.

She loses her voice for a moment and then the first gong sounds.

The Present: The seeds which received little radiation have grown to plants which are normal in appearance. The seeds which received moderate radiation gave rise to mutations such as double blooms, giant stems, and variegated leaves. The seeds closest to the gamma source were killed or yielded dwarf plants.

The second gong rings.

The Future: After radiation is better understood, a day will come when the power from exploding atoms will change the whole world we know.

With inspiration.

Some of the mutations will be good ones—wonderful things beyond our dreams—and I believe, I believe this with all my heart, THE DAY WILL COME WHEN MANKIND WILL THANK GOD FOR THE STRANGE AND BEAUTIFUL ENERGY FROM THE ATOM.

Part of her last speech is reverberated electronically. Deep pulses of music are added as the light focuses on TILLIE's *face.*

Suddenly there is silence, except for RUTH *picking up* TILLIE's *last words.*

The lights come up on the main set, and the room is empty.

RUTH *bursts in the front door. She is carrying the three-panel card and a shopping bag of plants, both of which she drops on the floor.*

RUTH: MAMA! MAMA! She won! Mama! Where are you? She won!

She runs back to the front door and yells to TILLIE.

Hurry up! Hurry! Oh, my God, I can't believe it!

Then yelling upstairs.

Mama! Come on down! Hurry!

TILLIE *comes in the front door, carrying the rest of her plants, and the large trophy.*

RUTH *takes the trophy.*

Give me that!

She starts upstairs.

Mama! Wait till you see this!

BEATRICE *appears at the top of the stairs. She has been drinking a great deal, and clings fast to a bunch of old cheap curtains and other material.*

Mama! She won . . .

BEATRICE *continues mechanically on down the stairs.*

Didn't you hear me? Tillie won the whole thing! . . . Mama? . . . What's the matter with you? What did you rip the paper off the windows for?

BEATRICE *commences tacking up one of the curtains.*

TILLIE: Mama? Are you going to open a . . . shop?

RUTH: What's the matter? Can't you even answer?

BEATRICE: *To* TILLIE.
Hand me some of those tacks.

RUTH: *Screaming.*
I SAID SHE WON! ARE YOU DEAF?

BEATRICE: Ruth, if you don't shut up I'm going to have you put away.

RUTH: They ought to put *you* away, BETTY THE LOON!

There is a long pause.

BEATRICE: The rabbit is in your room. I want you to bury it in the morning.

RUTH: If you did anything . . . I'LL KILL YOU!

She runs upstairs.

TILLIE: Mother, you didn't kill it, did you?

BEATRICE: Nanny goes tomorrow. First thing tomorrow.

There is a cry from upstairs.

TILLIE: Ruth? Are you all right?

BEATRICE: I don't know what it's going to be. Maybe a tea shop. Maybe not.

RUTH *appears in the doorway of her room. She is holding the dead rabbit*

*on the blue towel. As she reaches the
top of the stairs, she begins to moan
deeply.*

After school you're going to have
regular hours. You'll work in the
kitchen, you'll learn how to cook,
and you're going to earn your keep,
just like in any other business.

TILLIE *starts slowly up the stairs toward* RUTH.

TILLIE: *With great fear.*
Mama . . . I think she's *going to go.*

RUTH *commences to tremble.* TILLIE
speaks softly to her.

Don't go . . . don't go . . .

RUTH's *eyes roll in her head, and
the trembling of her body becomes
pronounced throbbing. She drops the
rabbit with the towel covering it.*

Help me! Mama! Help me!

BEATRICE: Snap out of it, do you hear me? RUTH, DON'T LET YOURSELF GO!

To TILLIE.

Help me get her downstairs!

By the time the trio reaches the bottom of the stairs, RUTH *is consumed by a violent convulsion.* BEATRICE *holds her down and pushes* TILLIE *out of the way.*

BEATRICE: *Screaming.*
Get the wooden spoon!

TILLIE *responds as* BEATRICE *gets* RUTH *onto a sofa. The convulsion runs its course of a full minute, then finally subsides.* TILLIE *gets a blanket and covers* RUTH.

TILLIE: Shall I call the doctor?

There is a long pause.

Shall I call the doctor?

BEATRICE: No. She'll be all right.

TILLIE: I think we should call him.

BEATRICE: I DIDN'T ASK YOU WHAT YOU THOUGHT! . . . We're going to need every penny to get this place open.

BEATRICE spreads a tablecloth on one of the tables and places a pile of old cloth napkins on it. She sits down and lights a cigarette.

TILLIE: *Picking up the rabbit on the stairs.* I'd better bury him in the backyard.

She starts out.

BEATRICE: Don't bury the towel.

TILLIE stops, sobs audibly, then gets control.

TILLIE: I'll do it in the morning.

She gently lays the rabbit near the door. She tucks RUTH *in on the couch and sits a few minutes by her sleeping sister.*

Music starts in softly as BEATRICE *continues folding napkins with her back to the others.*

There is the sound of someone at the curtained doorway, and NANNY *commences negotiating herself into the room. Slowly she advances with the tubular frame—unaware, desiccated, in some other land.*

BEATRICE: *Weakly.*
Matilda?

TILLIE: Yes, Mama?

BEATRICE: I hate the world. Do you know that, Matilda?

TILLIE: Yes, Mama.

BEATRICE: I hate the world.

The lights have started down, the music makes its presence known, and a spot clings to TILLIE. *She moves to the staircase and the rest of the set goes to black during the following speech. As she starts up the stairs her recorded voice takes over as in the opening of the play.*

TILLIE'S VOICE: *The Conclusion:* My experiment has shown some of the strange effects radiation can produce . . . and how dangerous it can be if not handled correctly.

Mr. Goodman said I should tell in this conclusion what my future plans are and how this experiment has helped me make them.

For one thing, the effect of gamma rays on man-in-the-moon marigolds has made me curious about the sun and the stars, for the universe itself must be like a world of great atoms —and I want to know more about it.

But most important, I suppose, my experiment has made me feel important—every atom in me, in everybody, has come from the sun —from places beyond our dreams. The atoms of our hands, the atoms of our hearts . . .

All sound out.

TILLIE *speaks the rest live—hopeful, glowing.*

Atom.
Atom.
What a beautiful word.

THE END

Format by Gloria Bressler
Set in 12 pt. Bodoni
Composed by American Book-Stratford Press, Inc.

HarperCollins Publishers

mub